F-15 EAGLES

BY JACK DAVID

BELLWETHER MEDIA · MINNEAPOLIS, MN

TM

Are you ready to take it to the extreme?
Torque books thrust you into the action-packed
world of sports, vehicles, and adventure. These books
may include dirt, smoke, fire, and dangerous stunts.
WARNING: read at your own risk.

Library of Congress Cataloging-in-Publication Data

David, Jack, 1968-
  F-15 Eagles / by Jack David.
      p. cm. – (Torque: military machines)
  Includes bibliographical references and index.
  Summary: "Amazing photography and engaging information explain the technologies and
capabilities of the F-15 Eagles. Intended for students in grades 3 through 7"–Provided by publisher.
  ISBN-13: 978-1-60014-203-1 (hardcover : alk. paper)
  ISBN-10: 1-60014-203-6 (hardcover : alk. paper)
  1. Eagle (Jet fighter plane)–Juvenile literature. I. Title.

  UG1242.F5D3466 2008
  623.74'64–dc22   2008019865

This edition first published in 2009 by Bellwether Media.

The photographs in this book are reproduced through the courtesy of the United States Department of
Defense.

Printed in the United States of America.

CONTENTS

THE F-15 EAGLE IN ACTION

Four F-15 Eagles soar over the desert. They are on patrol protecting a U.S. base. Suddenly, six enemy aircraft appear. They're headed toward the base. The F-15 pilots quickly turn to **intercept** the planes.

5

Two pilots lock on to the enemy targets. They fire heat-seeking Sidewinder **missiles**. The missiles streak through the sky. Two enemy planes explode as the missiles strike. The four remaining enemy aircraft break off the attack. The U.S. base is safe. The F-15s have done their job.

★ FAST FACT ★

The F-15 was the United States' best air-to-air fighter in the Gulf War. F-15s earned 34 of the 37 air-to-air victories for the United States.

FIGHTER PLANE

The F-15 Eagle is an air-to-air fighter plane in the United States Air Force. Its **mission** is to fight enemy aircraft in the air. These battles are called **dogfights**. The F-15 can attack bombers, cargo planes, and other military aircraft. Its speed, handling, and advanced weaponry make it one of the world's best fighters.

The first F-15s entered service in 1972. Over the years, faster and more powerful models have come out. The F-15E Strike Eagle entered service in 1988. This advanced model is a **dual-role** fighter. It's built for air-to-ground attacks as well as air-to-air fighting.

★ FAST FACT ★

The F-15 can reach speeds more than two-and-a-half times the speed of sound. That's more than 1,800 miles (2,898 kilometers) per hour!

WEAPONS
AND FEATURES

The F-15 Eagle needs a lot of firepower to defeat enemy aircraft. Its main gun is the M61A1 cannon. It can also carry eight air-to-air missiles. The AIM-9 Sidewinder is a powerful heat-seeking missile. It locks on to the hot fumes that come out of an enemy's engine. Other air-to-air missiles include the AIM-7 Sparrow and the AIM-120 Advanced Medium Range Air-to-Air Missile (AMRAAM).

The F-15E Strike Eagle also carries air-to-ground missiles and bombs. The GBU-28 "Bunker Buster" is one of its most powerful bombs. It weighs 5,000 pounds! The Strike Eagle also carries **laser-guided bombs (LGBs)**. Computers guide these bombs to targets marked by a laser beam.

The United States isn't the only nation to use F-15s. The militaries of Japan, Israel, and Saudi Arabia also fly F-15s.

F-15 EAGLE SPECIFICATIONS:

Primary Function: Air superiority

Length: 63.8 feet (19.4 meters)

Height: 18.5 feet (5.6 meters)

Weight: 31,700 pounds (14,379 kilograms)

Wingspan: 42.8 feet (13 meters)

Speed: 1,875 miles (3,018 kilometers) per hour

Range: 3,450 miles (5,552 kilometers)

F-15 MISSIONS

The F-15's primary function is **air superiority**. The F-15's job is to be better, faster, and stronger than any enemy plane. It can be used for attack or defense. It can patrol airspace. It can **escort** other planes such as bombers or cargo planes.

BT

AF 79 058

Each F-15 costs about $30 million.

Air Force personnel work together
to perform missions. In the Strike Eagle,
a **weapons specialist** joins the pilot.
The weapons specialist is in charge of
the air-to-ground weapons. The weapons
specialist and the pilot work together to
make their missions successful.

GLOSSARY

air superiority—the ability to counter any force in the air; the F-15's primary role is to control the air in any battle.

dogfight—an aerial battle between two or more fighter planes

dual-role—serving two main purposes

escort—to travel alongside and protect

intercept—to prevent something, such as a plane or missile, from reaching its target

laser-guided bomb (LGB)—an explosive that locks onto a target that has been marked with a laser

missile—an explosive launched at targets on the ground or in the air

mission—a military task

weapons specialist—the crew member of an F-15 Strike Eagle who is in charge of air-to-ground weapons

TO LEARN MORE

AT THE LIBRARY

Braulick, Carrie A. *U.S. Air Force Fighters*. Mankato, Minn.: Capstone, 2006.

Green, Michael and Gladys. *Tactical Fighters: The F-15 Eagles*. Mankato, Minn.: Capstone, 2008.

Zobel, Derek. *United States Air Force*. Minneapolis, Minn.: Bellwether, 2008.

ON THE WEB

Learning more about military machines is as easy as 1, 2, 3.

1. Go to www.factsurfer.com

2. Enter "military machines" into search box.

3. Click the "Surf" button and you will see a list of related web sites.

With factsurfer.com, finding more information is just a click away.

INDEX